EXTREME WEATHER

CHALLENGE YOURSELF

WEIRD TRIVIA AND UNBELIEVABLE FACTS TO TEST YOUR KNOWLEDGE ABOUT STORMS, CLIMATE, METEOROLOGY, & MORE!

JEFF PROBST

EXTREME WEATHER

CHALLENGE YOURSELF

Puffin Books

PUFFIN BOOKS
An imprint of Penguin Random House LLC
375 Hudson Street
New York, New York 10014

First published in the United States of America by Puffin Books,
an imprint of Penguin Random House LLC, 2017

LIBRARY OF CONGRESS CATALOGING-IN-PUBLICATION DATA IS AVAILABLE

ISBN 9780147518118 (hardcover)
ISBN 9780147518101 (paperback)

Printed in China

1 3 5 7 9 10 8 6 4 2

Designed by Maria Fazio

Photo Credits

Thinkstock: pages ii–iii, 10 (bottom image), 18–19, 26–27, 29 (small image), 41, 61, 68–69,
90, 106–109, 152, 158–159

Shutterstock: pages i, vi, 2–3, 5–11, 13–16, 20–23, 25, 28–34, 36–37, 39–40, 41 (top image),
42–59, 61 (top image), 63–65, 67, 70–73, 75–78, 80–87, 91–92, 94, 96, 98–104, 110–113,
115–116, 119–143, 146–147, 154–157, 160

iStock: pages 11 (bottom image), 35, 79, 82–83 (bottom image), 88–89, 97,
120 (small image), 150, 153

Wiki Commons: pages 93, 114–115, 144, 148–149, 151

All background patterns courtesy of Shutterstock: pages vi–1, 4, 10–17, 22–25,
34–35, 37–40, 54–55, 60–63, 66, 70–71, 74, 78, 80–81, 86–87, 90–93, 106 108–109, 114–115,
118, 122–123, 128–129, 132–133, 138–139, 148–157

All other photos courtesy of the author

I hereby dedicate this book to Alyssa & Evan!
You are both so amazing and so fun to be around.

Each time we are together you
make me laugh or teach me something new.

I look forward to our next adventure together!
Here's to the howler monkeys!

Uncle Jeff

Hey, young readers!

I learned so much as we were putting this book together. You ready for my big takeaway . . . ? Weather is really unpredictable . . . and in a weird, super-fun way! It's why going out to play in a rainstorm is irresistible. In fact, some of my favorite memories of *Survivor* are connected to crazy weather——a monstrous storm that comes out of nowhere or a blistering hot day when you are certain your skin is going to burn right off your body!

So leave the umbrella at home and enjoy what mother nature has to offer!

I hope you dig the book!!

Jeff Probst

Note to readers:
See a word in bold? Check out the glossary in the back to find out what it means!

WEATHER OR NOT . . .

What's it like outside today? Is it hot or cold? Bright or foggy? Is there a rainstorm approaching, with quaking thunderclaps? Or is it peaceful, without a cloud in the sky?

Weather is basically the condition of the **atmosphere** at a given time, including its effects on life on the ground. It describes conditions that last a relatively short period of time, ranging from a couple of minutes to sometimes even months.

Climate, on the other hand, describes longer-term patterns, such as average temperature or average rainfall in a given area.

The standard averaging period to determine climate is 30 years! Imagine having your temperature taken every day for that long.

CHALLENGE YOURSELF!

Which of the following is a type of climate?

A Tropical rain forest

B Dry desert

C Polar ice cap

D All of the above

ANSWER: **D!**
These are all examples of **climates**! According to one of the most widely used climate classification systems (developed by Russian German climatologist Wladimir Köppen in 1884), there are five primary climate classifications: tropical, dry, mild, continental, and polar.

DRY DESERT

POLAR ICE CAP

TROPICAL RAIN FOREST

5

CLIMATE ON EARTH

A place's **climate** is affected by its latitude, how high up it is, and what the ground is made of. Latitude is a measure of how far a place is from the **Equator**. Altitude is a measure of how high or low a place is compared to **sea level**. And terrain describes the surface of the land, such as if it is rocky or not. A place's climate is also affected by its closeness to bodies of water.

Climate is formed by an interactive system composed of the **atmosphere** (air), the hydrosphere (water), the cryosphere (ice), the lithosphere (land, which includes lava), and the biosphere, which is made up of various living organisms. The final component is the sun, which is climate's most important factor.

The sun's solar radiation heats the surface of the Earth, which in turn heats the atmosphere. When the sun heats up the water and land, the heat is transferred to the air, creating wind and other weather.

2-DAY + 2-MORROW = THE 4-CAST

Meteorology is the study of the **atmosphere**. Meteorologists are scientists who forecast, or predict, the weather based on the information available.

THE TOOLS OF PREDICTION

It's one thing to study the weather as it is. It's another thing entirely to forecast weather that hasn't happened yet! To do this, meteorologists use specialized instruments, along with mathematics, physics, and more, to make informed predictions concerning weather patterns.

Weather satellites take photographs that reveal and track events in the atmosphere. Weather maps display information about atmospheric conditions over a given area, allowing meteorologists to see the "big picture" of what is happening with the weather.

WEATHER SATELLITE

9

THERMOMETER
A thermometer measures the temperature of the air.

BAROMETER
A barometer measures **air pressure**, the weight of air in the **atmosphere** pressing down.

RAIN GAUGE
A rain gauge measures the amount of precipitation over a specific time period.

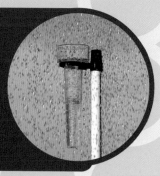

WIND VANE

A wind vane determines the direction from which the wind is blowing.

ANEMOMETER

An anemometer measures the wind's speed.

HYGROMETER

A hygrometer measures **humidity**, the amount of **water vapor** in the air.

WEATHER BALLOON

Weather balloons carry instruments into the **troposphere** and stratosphere to gather data on conditions high above the ground.

The sun heats the Earth unevenly, causing air and clouds in the **atmosphere** to move. Between that and the rotation of the Earth, which affects wind patterns, there is a lot of activity in the sky!

SINKING AIR DRIES

Because **air pressure** is greatest close to the ground, air compresses and its molecules collide more frequently. The change causes the sinking air to warm up, and the ice and water in the air to evaporate, drying it out.

AIR COOLS ON THE WAY UP

The atmosphere generally cools with height. The higher up in the atmosphere, the colder the air. As warm air rises, it cools off. **Water vapor** in the air condenses as the air cools, becoming liquid water or even solid ice crystals. This is part of the water cycle, the basic process responsible for rain, snow, and other **precipitation**.

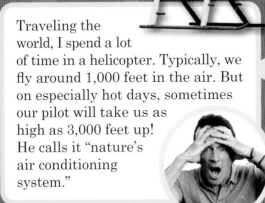

Traveling the world, I spend a lot of time in a helicopter. Typically, we fly around 1,000 feet in the air. But on especially hot days, sometimes our pilot will take us as high as 3,000 feet up! He calls it "nature's air conditioning system."

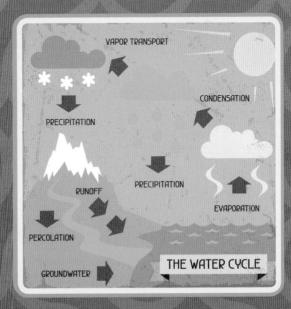

VAPOR TRANSPORT

CONDENSATION

PRECIPITATION

RUNOFF

PRECIPITATION

EVAPORATION

PERCOLATION

THE WATER CYCLE

GROUNDWATER

The **atmosphere** surrounds the Earth like a blanket and helps maintain livable temperatures by regulating the amount of radiation from the sun that reaches and leaves the planet.

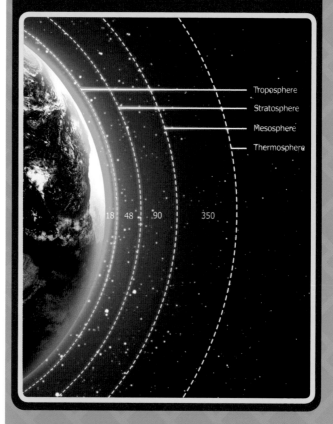

Troposphere
Stratosphere
Mesosphere
Thermosphere

18 48   90   350

The gases that form the atmosphere allow for life on Earth. These gases include nitrogen, oxygen, argon, and carbon dioxide. There is also **water vapor**, dust, and other particles.

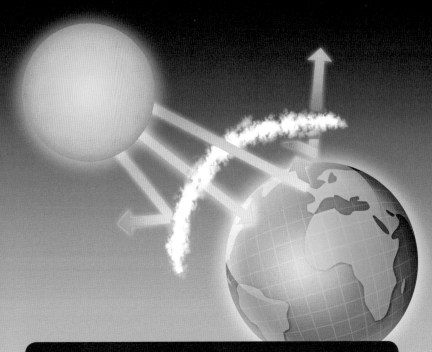

THE GREENHOUSE EFFECT

The atmosphere doesn't only block out **solar radiation**. It also traps it in! The sun's energy that penetrates the atmosphere is absorbed by the land, water, and plants. In a process called the greenhouse effect, special gases in the Earth's atmosphere absorb and re-emit radiation, and it bounces around, continuing to heat the planet.

It's called the greenhouse effect because it reminded people of sunlight entering the glass windows of a greenhouse. Without the greenhouse effect, the Earth would be too cold, even with sunlight, to sustain human life.

CRAZY BUT TRUE

Nitrogen makes up 78% of atmospheric gases!

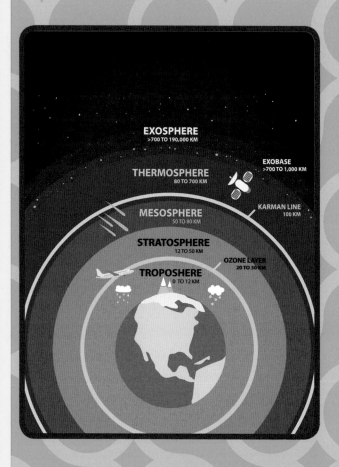

EXOSPHERE
>700 TO 190,000 KM

EXOBASE
>700 TO 1,000 KM

THERMOSPHERE
80 TO 700 KM

KARMAN LINE
100 KM

MESOSPHERE
50 TO 80 KM

STRATOSPHERE
12 TO 50 KM

OZONE LAYER
20 TO 30 KM

TROPOSPHERE
0 TO 12 KM

The **atmosphere** is divided into 5 main layers: the exosphere, the thermosphere, the mesosphere, the stratosphere, and the **troposphere**.

Air is thickest in the troposphere, the layer closest to the ground. It is also where the majority of weather occurs. The troposphere is 4 to 12 miles thick, and contains the air that plants and animals breathe.

The stratosphere is the second-closest layer to Earth. It is where planes fly, and extends as far as 31 miles up! The air in the stratosphere is a thousand times thinner than the air at **sea level**!

The mesosphere is the coldest layer of Earth's atmosphere. The average temperature is about −130°F. This is the layer where meteors often burn up as they fall to Earth.

The thermosphere is vast and hot, and it's sometimes thought of as the beginning of outer space. It starts 53 miles up and can spread 372 miles from the Earth's surface. Temperatures in the thermosphere soar to around 2,700°F or hotter!

The exosphere is the farthest layer. It contains very widely dispersed gas particles. It borders on the vacuum of outer space, and shares more qualities with space than with air. In fact, some scientists don't believe that it's part of the atmosphere at all!

TRICKS OF LIGHT

WHY IS THE SKY BLUE?

As the sun's light passes through the Earth's **atmosphere**, it is scattered by trillions of dust and gas molecules in the air. Because the **wavelength** of blue light is short, more blue light is scattered in all directions as it passes through the sky than any other color, giving the sky its blue appearance.

WHY IS A SUNSET RED?

Because red light has a longer wavelength, it doesn't scatter as easily as it passes through the atmosphere. As the sun sets, the sun's light has to pass a greater distance through the atmosphere to reach your eyes. As the sun gets lower the blue light has to pass through more and more air. It gets scattered so much that what's left is mostly red, orange, and yellow.

HOW HURRICANES ARE BORN

THE CORIOLIS EFFECT

Ocean storms form when areas of differing temperature come in contact with each other, causing a change in **air pressure**. Warm, moist air rises, cooling quickly, and as it does the water it carries condenses, forming rain-clouds. The air moves toward the center of the storm, going from areas of high pressure to low pressure. However, due to the rotation of the Earth, air is deflected to the right (in the Northern Hemisphere) or the left (in the Southern Hemisphere), causing the storm to form a spiraling shape. This deflecting force is called the Coriolis effect. Sometimes, the spiral creates a self-sustaining circle, and the storm is able to fuel itself, growing larger as it passes over the warm ocean surface. This is called a **tropical depression**.

SATELLITE VIEW OF A HURRICANE

21

A GROWING STORM

When a **tropical depression** has consistent wind gusts of 39 miles per hour or faster, it is called a tropical storm. And when the storm becomes strong enough to blow 74-mile-per-hour winds, it becomes a **hurricane**. These storms of wind and rain can last for longer than a week, moving slowly across the ocean as they grow larger and more intense.

TROPICAL STORM

Hurricanes can be up to 600 miles across, and can blow at speeds of more than 200 miles per hour!

HURRICANE DAMAGE

TRUE OR FALSE?
The central "eye" of the storm is where the strongest winds blow.

CHALLENGE YOURSELF!

ANSWER: False!
The eye of the storm is the calmest part and has only light surface winds due to the upward draft.

23

HOW STRONG CAN HURRICANES GET?

SAFFIR-SIMPSON HURRICANE SCALE

The Saffir-Simpson hurricane scale rates **hurricanes** from 1 to 5, based on their wind speed and intensity. Category 1 hurricanes cause the least damage. Category 2 hurricanes have winds up to 110 miles per hour and can blow down trees and break windows. Category 3 hurricanes have winds up to 129 miles per hour. They can flood escape routes, damage homes and public buildings, and water sources may be compromised. And Category 4 hurricanes have winds up to 156 miles per hour—strong enough to destroy mobile homes, trees, signs, and the roofs, windows, and doors of permanent buildings.

Category 5 hurricanes are the strongest and most dangerous. They have winds of more than 156 miles per hour! They are strong enough to blow the roofs off buildings. These massive storms can require evacuations of coastal towns, and often result in several casualties.

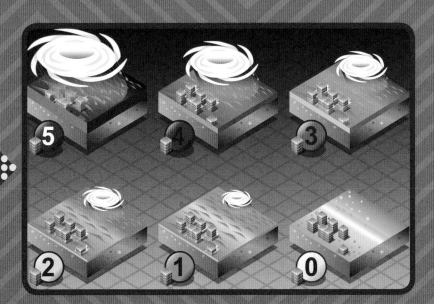

CRAZY BUT TRUE

Strong hurricanes are powerful enough that they're capable of creating spin-off tornadoes!

Tropical cyclones in the Pacific with wind gusts of 150 miles per hour or more are called super-typhoons!

THUNDER & LIGHTNING!

CHALLENGE YOURSELF!

TRUE OR FALSE?
**All lightning is
produced by a thunderstorm.**

ANSWER: **False!**
All thunderstorms have **lightning**. But lightning can still occur without rain. This is called dry lightning. Lightning can be witnessed in volcanic eruptions, during forest fires, at the site of nuclear detonations, and even in snowstorms.

Lightning is a huge spark of electricity discharged in the **atmosphere**, seen during thunderstorms. **Thunder** is the explosive sound made when lightning flashes, heating and expanding the air in an instant!

Did you know you can estimate how far away a lightning strike is by counting how many seconds pass between seeing it and hearing it? It's true! The light from the lightning travels almost instantly. But the sound of thunder takes approximately 5 seconds to travel 1 mile. Generally speaking, experts recommend taking cover if the "flash-to-bang" count time is less than 30 seconds—which means the lightning is striking less than 6 miles away! But while filming *Survivor* during a storm, our safety expert waits until a storm is as close as 1 mile away before suspending a shoot for our safety.

FROSTY FLAKES!

HOW SNOWFLAKES FORM

Snow forms when **water vapor** in the **atmosphere** condenses and freezes into ice crystals.

A single snowflake begins to form when a droplet of super-cold water freezes onto a particle in the atmosphere. This creates an ice crystal.

The ice crystal begins to fall through the air. As it does, water vapor freezes onto the primary crystal, adding new crystals to the design.

Snowflakes form a variety of different shapes, but all snowflakes have six sides.

WHEN IT RAINS, IT POURS.

CHALLENGE YOURSELF!

Which of the following is an example of precipitation?

A Rain

B Icicles

C Water from a sprinkler

D All of the above

ANSWER: **A!**
Rain, snow, sleet, and hail are all forms of **precipitation**, which falls to the ground from high up in the sky.

The **atmosphere** contains about 3.4 **millon billion** gallons of water! Most of it is in the form of **water vapor**.

Rainstorms can cause delays to outdoor activities, and can even cause serious damage. But if there's a silver lining in every cloud, it's that rainwater can also provide a legitimate source for drinking water. In fact, in many of the countries I travel to for *Survivor*, having a water-collection system is crucial to human survival. I've seen some pretty elaborate systems to collect and store rainwater for the use of the community. Some even use materials like bamboo to "harvest" rainwater.

WATER VAPOR ON A LAKE

RAINBOW COLORS

A rainbow is an arc of colors in the sky that appears when sunlight is broken up and reflected by water droplets.

CHALLENGE YOURSELF!

TRUE OR FALSE?
Double rainbows are real.

ANSWER: **True!**
Double rainbows occur when the sun is reflected twice through a raindrop instead of just once. Look closely and you'll see that the colors are reversed! Red appears on the inside of the arc.

CHALLENGE YOURSELF!

The colors of a rainbow appear in which order?

A Red, blue, yellow, orange, green, and gray

B Red, orange, yellow, green, blue, indigo, and violet

C Red, orange, yellow, blue, green, purple, and pink

ANSWER: **B!**

You can use the acronym Roy G Biv to remember the order of a rainbow's colors. This pattern is called a primary rainbow.

Rain Check!

DOPPLER RADAR

Doppler radar uses reflected microwave signals to determine the speed, or velocity, of a target. Police use Doppler radar in speed guns to determine if drivers are breaking the speed limit. Meteorologists use the same technology to check for rain clouds and to study storms. This is called weather surveillance radar (WSR).

CRAZY BUT TRUE

The use of radar to study the weather happened somewhat by accident. During World War II, military radar operators found that storms showed up while they were trying to detect enemy targets. Shortly after the war, meteorologists began using surplus radars to study rain clouds and other weather.

Today's radar technology is far more advanced. In addition to detecting **precipitation**, radars can distinguish what type of precipitation appears—even for storms very far away. There are satellites in space that systematically scan the globe. Some can even see through clouds, and are able to digitally map the inside of a storm like a CAT scan.

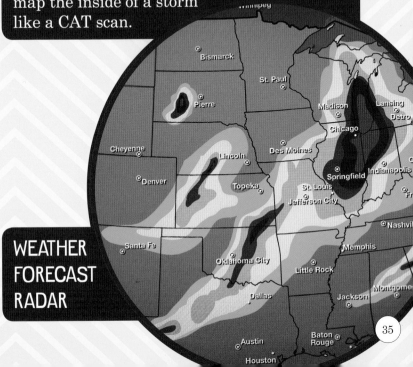

WEATHER
FORECAST
RADAR

Clouds are made of invisible **water vapor**, water droplets, and various impurities, like dust particles. Water vapor is the gaseous form of water. It is in all air, but especially warmer, humid air. There's water vapor in the air you breathe out, and even in a clear blue sky.

BRIGHT WHITE CLOUDS

Clouds can appear bright white, even when they're made mostly of invisible water vapor and very tiny droplets. That's because they scatter all **wavelengths** of light and reflect the bright white light of the sun!

STORM CLOUDS

Storm clouds, by comparison, are dark and gray. That's because they're made up of large water droplets or ice crystals instead of vapor. The visible liquid and solid water are thicker and denser, scattering more light and allowing less to reach your eyes.

TRUE OR FALSE?
Clouds can contain snowflakes, even in the summer.

CHALLENGE YOURSELF!

ANSWER: **True!**
The temperature high up in the **atmosphere** is very different than it is on the ground. Sometimes, the conditions for making snow are right, even if snowflakes would never survive all the way to the ground.

THE WATER CYCLE

CHALLENGE YOURSELF!

What is the part of the cycle called in which melting snow and falling rain flow back toward lakes and oceans?

 A Collision

 B Collection

 C Condensation

ANSWER: **B!**
Oceans, rivers, and lakes collect water that has fallen or melted. The water then evaporates as the cycle continues anew.

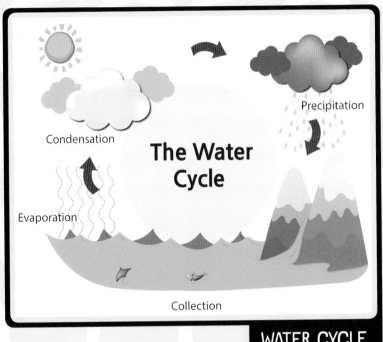

The Water Cycle

Condensation

Precipitation

Evaporation

Collection

As **water vapor** rises, the air cools and the vapor condenses into liquid and clings to tiny specks of dust and other impurities.

Water gathers on each dust particle until it forms a raindrop large and heavy enough to fall. Raindrops can fall at a speed of 7 to 18 miles per hour. In strong winds, they travel even faster!

Low-level clouds are among the most well known. They form less than 6,500 feet in the air, and include cumulus, stratocumulus, and stratus clouds.

Cumulonimbus clouds are the biggest clouds in the world and hold up to half a million tons of water!

Medium-level clouds form up to 23,000 feet in the **atmosphere**. They include altocumulus, altostratus, and nimbostratus.

High-level clouds are cirrus clouds. They include cirrocumulus and cirrostratus clouds as well. They can form upward of 40,000 feet in the air!

CRAZY BUT TRUE

Noctilucent clouds are the highest clouds in Earth's atmosphere. They form in the mesosphere, about 50 miles above the ground!

NOCTILUCENT CLOUDS

CIRROSTRATUS CLOUDS

ALTOCUMULUS CLOUDS

CUMULUS CLOUDS

GUST 'CAUSE

All air in the **atmosphere** is riding one wind or another. The air is never completely still. Wind happens when air moves from areas of high **air pressure** to low air pressure.

WIND DAMAGE

- Winds with speeds of 45 to 57 miles per hour can bend trees, break small or weak limbs, and damage homes.
- Winds with speeds of 58 to 74 miles per hour can break larger limbs, uproot young trees, and even overturn semitrucks!
- Winds with speeds of 75 to 89 miles per hour will do widespread damage to trees, roofs of buildings, and any weakened structures in their path.

CRAZY BUT TRUE

The fastest gust of wind ever recorded was on Barrow Island, Western Australia, on April 10, 1996. It blew an unimaginable 253 miles per hour. That's faster than the winds of some Category 5 **hurricanes**! Talk about blowing away the competition!

WINDY CITY

Chicago, Illinois, is nicknamed the Windy City, experiencing healthy gusts coming off Lake Michigan. But with an average wind speed of 10.3 miles per hour, Chicago isn't really the windiest city.

America's true Windy City is Amarillo, Texas! It has an average wind speed of 13.6 miles per hour, the fastest in the United States.

CHICAGO

CRAZY BUT TRUE

Amarillo's record wind speed was 84 miles per hour! The gust happened on May 15, 1949, when a tornado passed within 0.8 miles of the instruments used to take the measurement.

NORTHERN LIGHTS

Auroras are shimmering, colored lights caused by charged particles from the sun that glow as they enter the Earth's **atmosphere** and collide with particles there. Similar to how neon gas can light up to form bright colors in signs, these particles release light in the form of "photons" as they hit air molecules in the sky.

THE BRIGHTEST LIGHTS

Aurora borealis is the official name of what we commonly call the Northern Lights. Scientists now believe that auroral activity peaks every 11 years. If their calculations are correct, the year 2024 should be a particularly great year to catch a glimpse.

HEAT WAVES

A **heat wave** is a long period of very high heat, usually combined with high **humidity**. Heat waves usually happen during the summer months. They occur when high **air pressure** 10,000 to 25,000 feet up in the **atmosphere** stays in one area and traps heat near the ground.

THE MOST DEADLY WEATHER OF ALL!

Heat waves are the most lethal type of weather phenomenon. In fact, they kill more Americans than any other type of natural disaster. About 400 people a year die because of heat waves.

A heat wave in Europe in 2003 is credited with killing more than 70,000 people

Heat-related illnesses are preventable. During a heat wave, it's important to stay hydrated. Drink plenty of water! And eating a salty snack can help your body replace salt lost from sweating. On the set of *Survivor*, we take every precaution to make sure high temperatures, physical activity, and dehydration don't turn into a deadly combination.

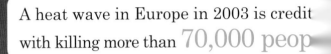

CRAZY BUT TRUE

It has been said that heat waves even increase a city's murder rate

AVALANCHE!

An avalanche is when a massive amount of snow and ice (and usually rocks and dirt) falls quickly down the side of a mountain.

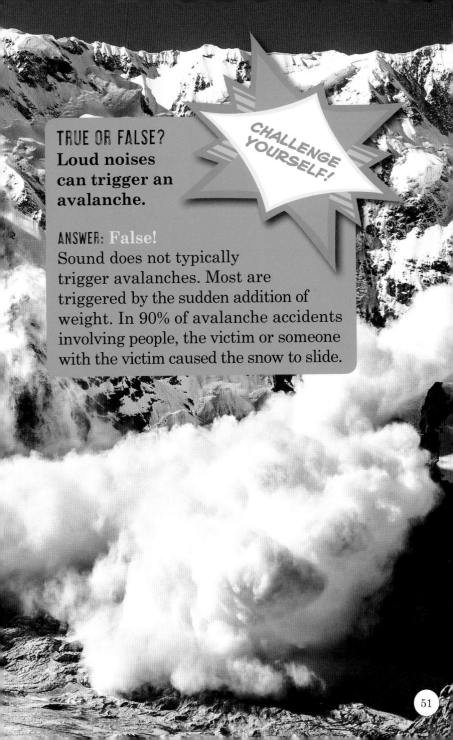

CHALLENGE YOURSELF!

TRUE OR FALSE?
Loud noises can trigger an avalanche.

ANSWER: False!
Sound does not typically trigger avalanches. Most are triggered by the sudden addition of weight. In 90% of avalanche accidents involving people, the victim or someone with the victim caused the snow to slide.

51

HOW DO YOU DEW?

Have you ever woken up to find the grass wet with tiny drops of water, even though it didn't rain? Those drops of water are called **dew**.

Sometimes, when the temperature drops suddenly (like it can at night), the **water vapor** in the air condenses and gathers on exposed surfaces. The temperature at which dew starts to form is called the **dew point**.

ICE CRYSTALS

Frost occurs when the dew point is below freezing. Instead of moisture gathering on surfaces as tiny drops of water, water vapor changes directly from a gas into a solid, in the form of ice crystals.

STORM WITH A TWIST

TORNADOES

Tornadoes are nature's most violent storms. These funnel-shaped clouds might be smaller than **hurricanes** and other storms, but their focused energy can do as much damage. Some tornadoes have wind speeds faster than 300 miles per hour! They can throw cars in the air, rip houses apart, and turn broken glass and other debris

About 1,200 tornadoes strike in the United States each year, more than anywhere else in the world!

CRAZY BUT TRUE

Scientists don't know exactly how fast the fastest internal winds of a tornado can be. The strongest tornadoes are so violent they actually destroy weather instruments. The strongest to be successfully recorded, however, was 318 miles per hour!

ASSESSING THE DAMAGE

Unlike **hurricanes**, which are given an intensity rating before they make landfall, tornadoes are rated only after the fact. The overall strength of a tornado is determined scientifically, based on the damage it caused. By analyzing debris, for example, scientists can estimate wind speeds.

The system for rating tornadoes is called the Enhanced Fujita (EF) scale. The most violent, destructive storms are rated EF5.

CRAZY BUT TRUE

Tornadoes can dig! There have been reports of tornadoes having created trenches 3 feet deep and even having stripped asphalt off the ground!

TORNADO DESTRUCTION

GIANT WAVES!

Tsunami are seismic sea waves, caused by underwater earthquakes, **landslides**, or volcanic eruptions. They are much larger than normal waves and are super-fast. Tsunami waves can also be made by meteorites colliding with Earth or other disturbances that displace large amounts of water.

When shooting *Survivor*, we always have a detailed evacuation plan in case of a tsunami. We've rented local school buses and had them on standby to get us out of base camp, if necessary. Once, we even had the top floor of a casino renovated to house our entire crew! We've been very lucky, and we've never been on location when a tsunami hit. But in both Samoa and the Philippines, we wrapped production up only days before tragedy struck the very islands where we were shooting. I've seen firsthand the kind of devastation tsunami can leave in their wake. They can literally wipe out a community, taking many lives in the process.

CRAZY BUT TRUE

Tsunami can be more than a hundred feet tall and can move fast enough to outrace a commercial jet!

No Surfing!

Unlike most waves, which are propelled along the surface of water by wind and friction, **tsunami** are mostly deep underwater. A typical tsunami wouldn't be more than 3 feet high until it rapidly approaches the shore.

As the huge wave reaches shallow water, it slows down to about 30 miles per hour. The compression of the energy forces a wave up high into the air.

A tsunami can look like a wall of water as it approaches, but when it hits the shore a typical tsunami arrives as a series of fast, powerful floods.

SWEPT OUT TO SEA

Because tsunami can strike without warning, they are usually quite deadly. Flooding and propelled debris make the immediate shoreline the most dangerous place to be. Anything within a mile off shore, or fewer than 50 feet above **sea level**, is subject to immediate flooding.

The world's deadliest tsunami struck in 2004 and killed an estimated 283,000 people in 14 countries bordering the Indian Ocean.

TSUNAMI AFTERMATH

Weather fronts are boundaries between distinct **air masses** with conflicting characteristics. The word *front* comes from war, where opposing armies would meet along a battle line called a front.

A cold front is the leading edge of a colder, drier mass of air moving to replace a warmer air mass. On a weather map, a cold front is indicated by a blue line with blue barbs, like arrows, indicating what direction it is moving in.

Similarly, a warm front is the leading edge of a warmer, more humid mass of air. On a weather map, a warm front is indicated by a red line with red half circles.

When a cold front takes over an area of warm air, it forces the warm air upward, which may cause thunderstorms. When a warm front takes over, it climbs slowly on top of the cooler air and may cause rain followed by warmer temperatures.

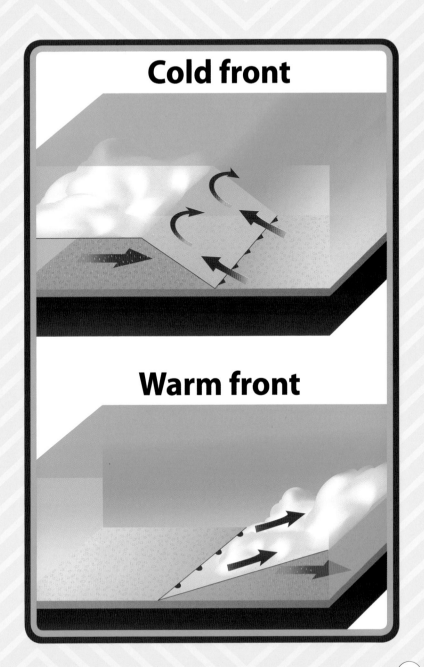

Cold front

Warm front

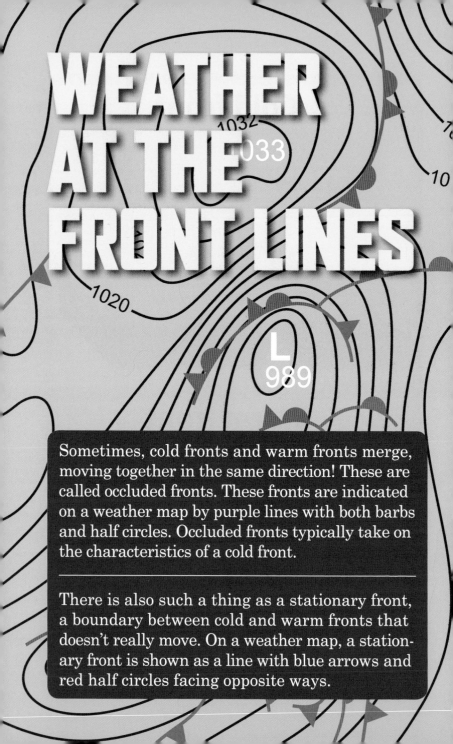

WEATHER AT THE FRONT LINES

1032
1033
10
1020

L
989

Sometimes, cold fronts and warm fronts merge, moving together in the same direction! These are called occluded fronts. These fronts are indicated on a weather map by purple lines with both barbs and half circles. Occluded fronts typically take on the characteristics of a cold front.

There is also such a thing as a stationary front, a boundary between cold and warm fronts that doesn't really move. On a weather map, a stationary front is shown as a line with blue arrows and red half circles facing opposite ways.

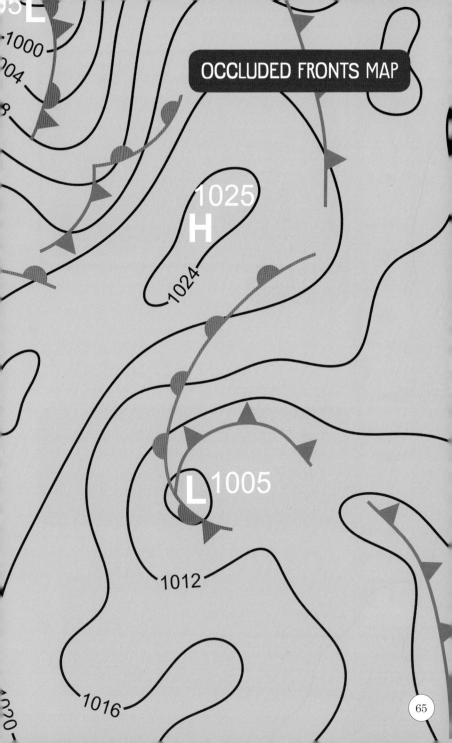

OCCLUDED FRONTS MAP

1025
H

1024

L 1005

1012

1016

1000
004
8

L

65

FIRENADO

What do you get when you mix a fire and a tornado? That's right. A firenado!

Researchers first documented the process, called pyro-tornadogenesis, after analyzing evidence from a wildfire in 2003. The 1,600-foot-wide fire whirl was seen moving at 160 miles per hour!

CRAZY BUT TRUE

Another extremely lethal firenado is believed to have killed 38,000 people in Japan—all in only 15 minutes!

The stuff of nightmares, a **fire whirl** is a spinning vortex of flame capable of reaching temperatures of up to 2,000°F. That's hot enough to turn ground ashes back into fuel.

Fire whirls form when winds converge on a flame. The super-heated air rises, pulling more wind and combustible gases into itself and causing the flame to turn and burn even more rapidly, sometimes well over 100 feet into the air.

These twisters are as dangerous as they sound. Even though fire whirls generally form when wind speeds are less than 20 miles per hour, they can generate the wind speeds of an EF2 tornado (111 to 135 mph), uprooting trees, tossing cars, and tearing—while searing— the roofs off buildings!

THE BEAUTY OF CLOUDS

CHALLENGE YOURSELF!

How long do clouds last, on average?

A 10 minutes

B 10 hours

C 10 days

ANSWER: A!

The average cloud lasts only about 10 minutes. But the life span of clouds can vary greatly. Some, such as man-made clouds, can last for only a few seconds. Some stratiform varieties can remain in the sky for many hours—or even days!

If you love clouds, you're not alone. The Cloud Appreciation Society is a membership organization dedicated to clouds. It has members from many different countries around the world. They urge people to "live life with your head in the clouds!"

The Cloud Appreciation Society gathers images of clouds from all over the globe. Their online gallery includes more than 11,000 pictures of clouds, and no two look exactly alike!

Clouds can shape-shift quickly! While shooting for *Survivor: Cambodia*, we had a special camera mounted on our helicopter, which was used to catch weather videos for the show. Sometimes, we would lock on a particularly beautiful cloud, and head straight for it! But by the time we got there, only a few minutes later, often the cloud had already changed formation.

Cloudy Skies

CLOUD SHAPES
Some clouds look like familiar animals and objects. Clouds can form in the shapes of smiling faces, teddy bears, whales, ducks, swans, question marks, sea horses, giants, butterflies, hearts, poodles, and many more!

Most clouds in the sky are found in the **troposphere**, the layer of the **atmosphere** closest to Earth. After all, that is where the vast majority of **water vapor** and dust can be found.

TRUE OR FALSE?
Fog is a type of cloud.

ANSWER: **True!**
Fog is a kind of cloud near or touching the ground. Sometimes, fog forms when mild, moist air flows over coastal inlets. The water vapor in the air condenses as it passes over the colder water or ground. Fog, by definition, is an area of low visibility. If you can see through it for more than 3,300 feet, it isn't actually fog, but mist.

Gravity holds the gases in air down just like it does objects on the ground. Cold air weighs more than warm air, which causes it to sink. This is because the molecules are held closer together. As air gets warmer, it floats upward. That's why a hot-air balloon works, floating high above the ground.

CHALLENGE YOURSELF!

Where did the word *hurricane* come from?

A The word *hurry*

B A Native American god of wind and storms

C Lake Huron

ANSWER: B!
Hurricanes get their name from the Mayan god Hurakan, the god of wind, fire, and storms.

Hurricanes don't form at the **Equator** where the surface water of the ocean is hottest. That's because it's also where the force of the Coriolis effect is weakest. The spiraling motion a hurricane needs in order to form happens only when conditions occur at least 5 degrees of latitude north or south of the Equator.

SATELLITE VIEW OF A HURRICANE

RAIN, RAIN, GO AWAY

MOUNT WAI'ALE'ALE

Mount Wai'ale'ale in Hawaii has been named one of the rainiest places on Earth. It rains on average 360 days a year. That means there are only 5 days a year it *doesn't* rain!

On average, Hawaii gets over 63 inches of rain each year. It is easily the rainiest place in the United States. Nevada gets only 9.5 inches of rain each year, making it the driest state.

RECORD-BREAKING RAINFALL

During a heavy storm on January 8, 1966, it rained 71.9 inches in Foc-Foc, La Réunion, an island in the Indian Ocean. That's the most rainfall ever recorded in a single day.

The most rain recorded in a single year happened in Cherrapunji, India. There, it rained more than 1,041 inches between August 1, 1860, and July 31, 1861.

While it doesn't rain that much every year, very heavy rain is typical in India from July to September. They call the season their rainy or wet season. The change is caused by a monsoon, a humid seasonal wind that carries huge amounts of **water vapor** from the southwest Indian Ocean.

Monsoons

The word *monsoon* comes from the Arabic word *mausim*, which means "wind" or "season." A monsoon is essentially a very large sea breeze, a wind that blows from a cool body of water over warmer land. It is typically accompanied by rainfall.

In some cases, monsoons are responsible for turning dry desert areas into lush, green grassland. Cultures throughout the world depend on the wet season to grow crops and feed communities.

But monsoons can also be dangerous. Heavy rain of any kind can lead to flooding and **mudslides**, a type of **landslide** in which rapidly moving water and debris can bury people and buildings in mud.

In 2005, India's monsoon season was so strong that more than $1,000$ people died in its storms, including flooding and mudslides.

LIGHTNING STRIKES

Stormy weather is generally accompanied by massive bolts of **lightning**. Between 10% and 30% of people struck by lightning don't survive. And up to 80% of those who do sustain long-term injuries.

FLASH FLOODS

Heavy rain can cause flash floods and **landslides**. Monsoon storms also cause downburst winds, lightning, and **thunder**.

Some flash floods happen when heavy rain makes water levels rise quickly. In the United States, flash floods kill more people than tornadoes, earthquakes, or lightning.

ACID RAIN

Another dangerous form of rain comes from pollution. Exhaust from factories and power stations goes up into the air. These pollutants react with water molecules to produce harmful, acidic rain. Unlike dust and dirt, which wash safely into the soil, **acid rain** can poison plants and animals—including humans.

The two Russian towns of Oymyakon and Verkhoyansk are tied for the coldest places on Earth in which people actually live. Each recorded lows of −90°F! In Oymyakon, schools stay open through weather as cold as −60°F!

CRAZY BUT TRUE

The coldest temperature ever recorded on Earth was in Antarctica. It was −128°F. That's colder than dry ice!

I grew up snow skiing in the Colorado Rockies, where it can be as cold as 0°F. And I thought *that* was cold!!!

OYMYAKON

FROZEN RIVER NEAR VERKHOYANSK

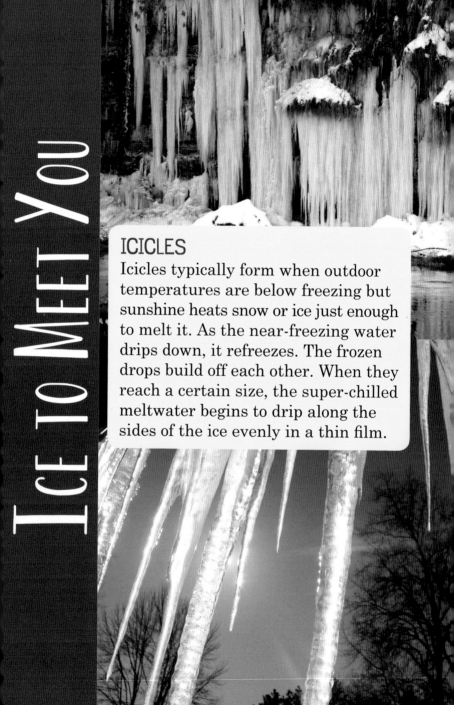

ICICLES

Icicles typically form when outdoor temperatures are below freezing but sunshine heats snow or ice just enough to melt it. As the near-freezing water drips down, it refreezes. The frozen drops build off each other. When they reach a certain size, the super-chilled meltwater begins to drip along the sides of the ice evenly in a thin film.

CAUTION! FALLING SPIKES!
Icicles can grow to yards long, but eventually they crash to the ground—either from melting or growing too large. Some can be very dangerous when they fall.

CHALLENGE
YOURSELF!

TRUE OR FALSE?
Tornadoes are unpredictable.

ANSWER: True!
The process by which tornadoes
form is still not entirely under-
stood. People cannot yet predict
exactly when or where tornadoes
will develop, how strong they'll be,
or even what path they are likely
to follow once they've formed.

That said, scientists can identify
the general conditions that lead to
tornado formation.

MESOCYCLONE

Doppler radar can detect a large rotating updraft inside a storm. Called **mesocyclones**, these large updrafts can be 1 to 6 miles wide, much larger than a tornado. But mesocyclones can provide conditions that allow tornadoes to form.

KILLER LIGHTNING

Florida is the undisputed Lightning
Capital of the United States. One
area of central Florida, stretching
from Tampa to Titusville, has so
much **lightning** it has been given
the nickname Lightning Alley!

How many volts of electricity does lightning discharge?

A 1 million

B 10 million

C 100 million

ANSWER: **C!**
Lightning discharges about 100 million volts of electricity. And yet, incredibly, people can and do survive being struck by lightning.

CRAZY BUT TRUE

Rwanda, Africa, is the Lightning Capital of the world. It receives almost 2.5 times the amount of lightning as Florida!

The largest snowstorms can drop
40 million tons of snow!

It snows an average of 57.87 feet
a year in Sukayu Onsen, Japan.
That's more than anywhere else
in the world! Some years it snows
over 70 feet!

Japan is also home to the
world's snowiest major city. The
city of Sapporo has a population
of more than a million people—
and an average yearly snowfall
of 234.24 inches
(19.52 feet)!

JAPAN

For comparison's sake, the most
it has ever snowed in 1 year in
Chicago was 89.7 inches.

THE MOUNT BAKER SKI AREA

The Mount Baker Ski Area outside of the town of Bellingham, Washington, received more than 95 feet of snow during the winter of 1998–1999 alone! It holds the current world record for highest total snowfall in a single year.

ALL IN A DAY'S WORK

The largest single snowstorm occurred in 1959. The Mount Shasta Ski Bowl in California received 15 feet 9 inches of snow over six days. It blanketed not only the ground but also the trees and houses.

Generally speaking, **drought** is a period of less-than-average **precipitation**. Droughts happen when places that are accustomed to having rain or snow don't receive the water they're used to.

CALIFORNIA'S STATE OF EMERGENCY

In 2014, California experienced the third driest year out of 119 years of statewide precipitation records. More than 80% of California was classified as being in "extreme" drought. In 2015, the federal government devoted millions in funding for drought relief projects in the state. Scientists estimate it would take 11 trillion gallons of water to solve California's water shortage.

THE DUST BOWL

During the 1930s, the United States suffered one of the worst droughts in its history. And it lasted for nearly a decade! About 80% of the country received less-than-average rain and snow, which along with strong winds and high temperatures caused more than 50 million acres of land to dry up. The Great Plains turned into a massive "dust bowl" of sand and dry soil, and crops dried up, too. By 1940, 2.5 million people had fled what had once been prosperous farmland.

BUBBLE BEACH!

Sea foam is a natural by-product of waves. As seawater churns, it can naturally foam up, due to dissolved organic matter in the water.

Though it's rare, there have been several cases in which sea foam builds up until the shoreline overflows with bubbles. In some extreme cases, the foam can be 10 feet high! Scientists credit the foamy phenomena to mysteriously high amounts of foaming agents, combined with heavier-than-normal waves—such as those following a storm.

Though either pollution or natural plant-based compounds could be responsible for the most extreme foam pileups, scientists do not believe the bubbles to be dangerous to the touch. The hazards of sea foam have more to do with its ability to conceal large rocks and storm debris than its being poisonous.

Unfortunately, evidence also shows that wild-life can be negatively impacted by prolonged exposure to the bubbles. Sea foam has been shown to de-waterproof bird feathers, leaving them vulnerable to the cold.

WEIRD LIGHTNING

Sometimes **lightning** appears to strike from the ground up!

LIGHTNING PHENOMENA!

Sometimes confused with lightning occurring in the upper **atmosphere**, sprites is the name for reddish-orange flashes high above thunderclouds. Sprites aren't actually lightning, but discharges of light triggered by other lightning.

St. Elmo's Fire is a weather phenomenon in which planes and ships can emit lightning-like sparks when traveling through bad weather. Because the phenomenon often happened at the end of a storm, sailors believed it to be a sign that their patron saint was protecting them.

BALL LIGHTNING

Ball lightning takes the form of a bright, hissing orb that moves around or hovers in place for only a few seconds before vanishing—sometimes with an explosive bang and sometimes making no sound at all.

Witnesses have described ball lightning for hundreds of years, and some have even caught their accounts on video. Still, scientists can only speculate on what might have caused the rare—and sometimes dangerous—light displays.

MEGATSUNAMI

Megatsunami are **tsunami** that have extraordinarily high waves and are usually caused by something falling into the water and displacing it, rather than underwater activity, as with most tsunami.

In 1958, one tsunami in Alaska was 1,720 feet high! It was created by a landslide caused by an earthquake that pushed 90 million tons of rock and ice into the bay.

It was the highest wave ever recorded!

PATH OF DESTRUCTION

Tornadoes can cross boundaries, like rivers and mountain slopes. Every major river east of the Rocky Mountains has been crossed by at least one significant tornado. And in 1987, one rare high-altitude tornado even managed to cross the Continental Divide in Wyoming's Yellowstone National Park!

CHALLENGE YOURSELF!

Which of the following is another name for a tornado?

 A Cyclone

 B Twister

 C Whirlpool

ANSWER: **B!**

Some people call tornadoes twisters! Because a tornado has a cyclonic circulation, in the past people referred to them as cyclones. But modern **meteorology** limits the use of the term *cyclone* to refer to larger circulations, like **hurricanes**.

EXTREME SNOWSTORMS!

Blizzards are huge snowstorms. They are categorized by prolonged winds with speeds of 35 miles per hour or more, heavy snowfall, and reduced visibility. They usually rage for more than 3 hours, and can cause mountains of snow, called **snowdrifts**, to form.

A ground blizzard is a snowstorm in which the snow in the air isn't falling but blows up off the ground due to strong winds. Both blizzards and ground blizzards can cause whiteout conditions, where visibility is near zero and you may not be able to see things right in front of you.

The first blizzard to be declared a federal emergency in the United States struck upstate New York and Southern Ontario in 1977. The storm accumulated several feet of snow, and the winds were deadly. Nearly 30 people died in the storm.

GLITTER IN THE CLOUDS!

HALOS

Halos can form in the sky, usually around the sun or moon. They are created by tiny ice crystals suspended in the atmosphere, usually in thin, high clouds.

Light pillars, sun dogs, and parhelic circles are all types of halos. Light pillars usually appear when the sun is near the horizon. Sun dogs, or phantom suns, appear on either side of the sun. And a parhelic circle can appear as a horizontal white line crossing through the sun.

It's important to always take precautions when observing any sun-related phenomena. Never look directly into the sun. The coating of the eyeball can get sunburned from the sun's ultraviolet light, causing painful blisters just like on the skin. And prolonged exposure can permanently damage the retina. Always wear protective glasses or use objects to shield your eyes from direct sunlight.

WORLD'S LARGEST SNOWFLAKES

Most snowflakes are less than half an inch across. Under the right conditions, unusually large snowflakes can form. Some of them are 3 to 4 inches across.

But the largest snowflake on record fell from the sky in Fort Keogh, Montana, in 1887. It was an incredible 15 inches wide and 8 inches thick. That's bigger than a sheet of notebook paper and as thick as a mattress!

CHALLENGE YOURSELF!

TRUE OR FALSE?
No two snowflakes are exactly the same.

ANSWER: True!
The pattern of ice crystals is determined by water molecules as they slow down. As a snowflake falls, the conditions it grows in fluctuate, slightly altering its pattern. Since every individual snowflake has an individual journey, no two patterns would have an identical design.

CRAZY BUT TRUE

Scientists who study ice crystallization have tried to make identical snowflakes in a lab setting, but to date none have been entirely successful.

Hurricane Katrina

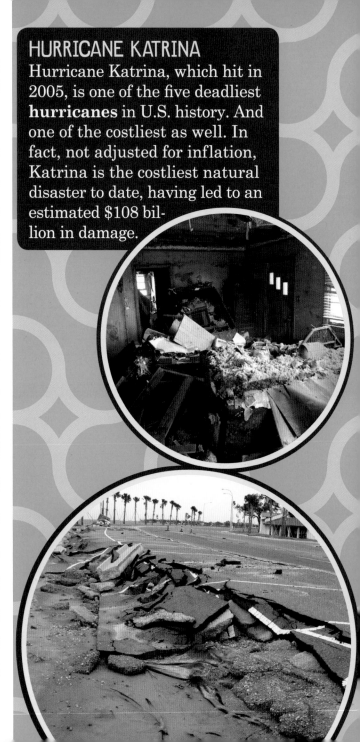

HURRICANE KATRINA

Hurricane Katrina, which hit in 2005, is one of the five deadliest **hurricanes** in U.S. history. And one of the costliest as well. In fact, not adjusted for inflation, Katrina is the costliest natural disaster to date, having led to an estimated $108 billion in damage.

A FLOODED CITY

The city of New Orleans sits below **sea level**. It relies on a system of **levees** to keep from flooding. But due to a catastrophic failure of the city's protection system, 80% of the city flooded during and after Hurricane Katrina. In some places the water was as much as 20 feet deep! Worse, the floodwaters lingered for weeks, long after the storm had passed.

At least 1,836 people died in the storm and subsequent floods. More than half of Katrina's victims were senior citizens who were unable to evacuate their homes.

Over 1 million people were displaced by Katrina. All told, the hurricane affected more than 15 million people and impacted 90,000 square miles of land.

WORLD'S WORST FLOODS

MISSISSIPPI RIVER

The most devastating river flood in U.S. history took place in 1927 when the Mississippi River overflowed, submerging about 26,000 square miles of land across Illinois, Missouri, Kentucky, Tennessee, Arkansas, Mississippi, Texas, Oklahoma, Kansas, and Louisiana. About 250 people were killed and about 600,000 others lost their homes.

AUSTRALIA

In 2010–2011, one the worst natural disasters in Australia's history took the form of a record-breaking series of floods that lasted for two months. They submerged 90 towns and cities and changed the lives of more than 200,000 people. The flood zone was the size of Germany and France combined!

The Smell of Rain

RAIN WASHES THE SKY

Have you ever noticed how clean the air smells after a long storm? Since raindrops form around dust and other impurities, when the rain falls down, dust falls with it. Without rain to pull impurities out of the air, the air would stay very dusty!

But cleanliness isn't all you smell when it rains. Your nose also picks up on two distinct scents: **ozone** and petrichor.

You can catch a whiff of the chemical ozone as a storm approaches. **Lightning** creates ozone (though it is also produced in the upper atmosphere), which has a distinct smell. In fact, ozone gets its name from the Greek word for *smell*.

When rain falls, a mix of chemicals called petrichor is released from the soil. Petrichor has an earthy smell, since it is produced from decomposed organic matter.

HAWAII

Hawaii has been hit by both local **tsunami** and tsunami that originated far away. The most disastrous of them struck in 1946, killing 159 people and creating $26 million worth of property damage.

ALASKA

Being near a major earthquake zone, Alaska has also suffered many tsunami. The most remarkable was generated by an intense earthquake in the Gulf of Alaska in 1964. The event created a Pacific-wide tsunami, and coastal **landslides** created localized tsunami as well.

IT'S TSUNAMI'S FAULT!

An underwater fault line runs from northern Vancouver Island, Canada, to Cape Mendocino, California. It is the kind of fault that could potentially cause an intense earthquake at any moment. Such an event would certainly trigger a tsunami. People along the 700-mile-long coast of Northern California, Oregon, and Washington would have between 15 and 30 minutes to escape.

Ninety-five thousand people live in tsunami zones on the U.S. West Coast. And an additional 42,000 people work there. All told, more than 100,000 people are at risk of a major tsunami strike in the United States right now.

QUALITIES OF LIGHTNING

A single bolt of **lightning** can travel 220,000 miles per hour and heat the air it touches to 54,000°F. That's at least three times hotter than the surface of the sun!

CRAZY BUT TRUE

There are around 3.6 billion lightning strikes per year. Approximately 25 million of them strike in the United States.

CHALLENGE
YOURSELF!

How thick and how long can a lightning bolt be?

A 1 foot in diameter and 1 mile long

B 1 inch in diameter and 100 miles long

C Scientists still don't know

ANSWER: **B!**
Lightning is only about 1 inch in diameter, and lightning bolts have been observed to be more than 100 miles long.

Typically, tornadoes travel only 10 to 20 miles per hour, though they can travel at least 3 times faster if the conditions are right.

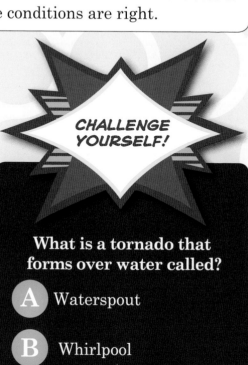

CHALLENGE YOURSELF!

What is a tornado that forms over water called?

A Waterspout

B Whirlpool

C These don't really exist

ANSWER: **A!**
Waterspouts can form above lakes and oceans. Some can be as dangerous as land tornadoes. Waterspouts can even move onto land, becoming normal tornadoes.

The average life span of a tornado is about 5 minutes. But tornadoes can last anywhere from an instant to several hours.

RAINING CATS & DOGS — & FISH?

RAINING SHARKS?!

In 2012, employees at the San Juan Hills Golf Club in California reported a leopard shark that fell from the sky near the 12th hole! Later, scientists figured out that it was carried high up into the sky by a bird, which later dropped it over the golf course.

Believe it or not, it's actually rained animals! Though it has never rained cats or dogs, it has rained toads, frogs, flounder, minnows, eels, snails, crayfish, maggots, pond mussels, and jellyfish. But how?

Scientists believe that **waterspouts** might be to blame. Every so often, they pull living things up out of the water and high up into the **atmosphere**. When the animals fall again, they are often far from the lake or pond they were snatched from.

In 2014, villagers in west Sri Lanka were thrilled when it rained 110 pounds of small edible fish! The prized creatures had been lifted out of a faraway river.

SNOW PLACE LIKE HOME!

IGLOOS

Houses or huts made of snow are called igloos. They typically have a domed roof and are made out of compressed snow, like the snow used to build a snowman. They are most often built and used as temporary shelter, such as during a hunting trip. Some even use crystal-clear ice for windows!

The air pockets in snow make it an effective insulator. Temperatures inside an igloo can get up to 61°F, even when outside temperatures are as low as −49°F!

The word *igloo* comes from the Inuit word *iglu*, which actually refers to a house or home made of any building material.

BIGLOO!

One of the largest snow igloos in the world, nicknamed the Bigloo, was constructed by three friends in Bellevue, Wisconsin, in 2010. The completed structure stood 17 feet 4 inches tall and 27 feet wide! It took 3 months to build. Each block of snow weighed between 60 and 100 pounds.

Another large igloo was built in Grand Falls, New Brunswick, Canada, in 2011—though it was made of blocks of ice instead of compacted snow.

TORNADO ALLEY

Tornadoes occur mostly during the spring and early summer in the central plains of North America, east of the Rocky Mountains and west of the Appalachian Mountains.

I grew up in Wichita, Kansas, where tornadoes were a fairly regular occurrence. I could always tell when one was coming, because the weather would get very calm. When it did, we would race outside to put our bikes in the garage so they wouldn't be swept away! Then my family members and I would head to our basement to wait out the storm.

NATURAL DISASTERS

In 2012, there were 905 natural disasters confirmed all around the world. And 93% of them were weather related.

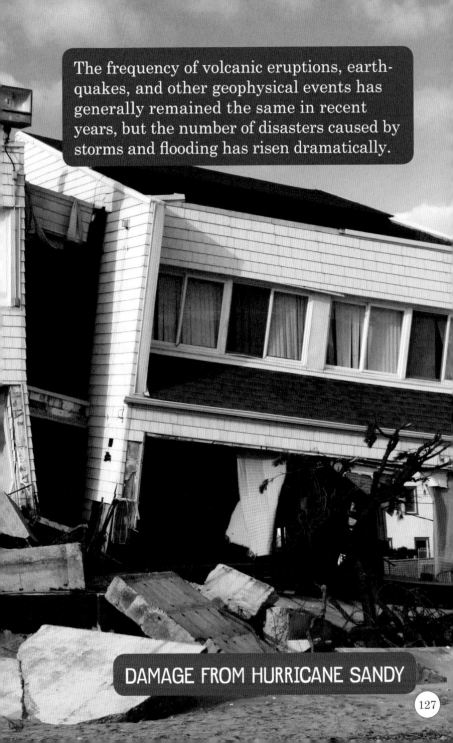

The frequency of volcanic eruptions, earthquakes, and other geophysical events has generally remained the same in recent years, but the number of disasters caused by storms and flooding has risen dramatically.

DAMAGE FROM HURRICANE SANDY

HURRICANE HUNTERS

Special planes are designed to fly straight into **hurricanes**! These aircraft operators are called hurricane hunters. They are part of the U.S. military. Their purpose is to gather important data about the storms, usually by crossing through a hurricane's eye several times per mission.

CRAZY BUT TRUE

As potentially hazardous as these missions are, very few aircrews have been lost since the program started during World War II.

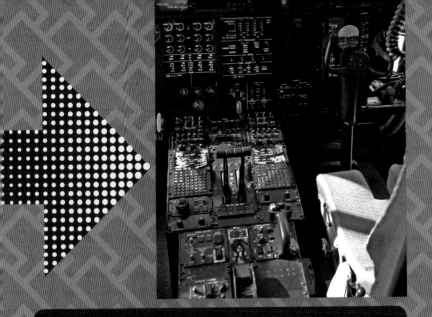

The weather these brave pilots face is so intense, they don't even bother bringing parachutes! They do, however, carry life preservers and inflatable rafts.

PROJECT STORMFURY

From 1962 to 1983, the U.S. government engaged in attempts to use hurricane hunters to weaken **tropical cyclones** before they grew into hurricanes. They used a process called **cloud seeding**, which introduces special particles to clouds to force them to rain or to suppress fog. In Project Stormfury, crews seeded clouds with silver iodide, hoping to disrupt the storms' inner structures.

When the theory behind Project Stormfury was proven false, the project was abandoned. However, scientists continue to investigate ways of weakening potentially disastrous weather.

SNOW MUCH SNOW!

Snow permanently or temporarily covers more than 20% of the Earth's surface, including 12% of the Earth's land surface. That's 39 million square miles!

Eighty percent of the world's fresh water is locked up as ice or snow. That's 7 million cubic miles!

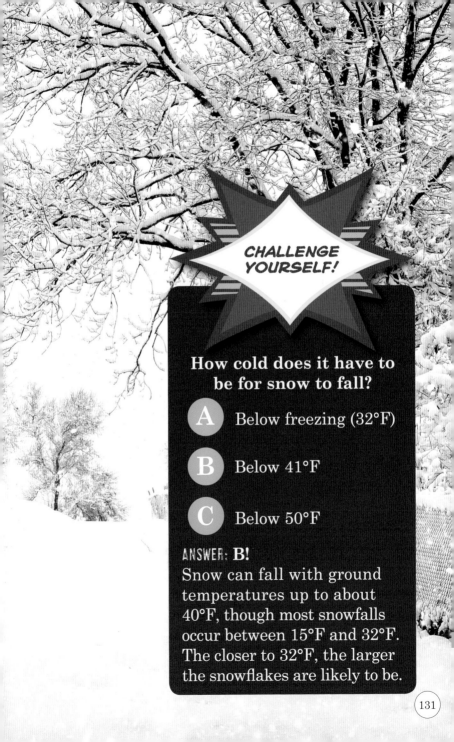

**How cold does it have to
be for snow to fall?**

A Below freezing (32°F)

B Below 41°F

C Below 50°F

ANSWER: **B!**
Snow can fall with ground
temperatures up to about
40°F, though most snowfalls
occur between 15°F and 32°F.
The closer to 32°F, the larger
the snowflakes are likely to be.

COLORFUL LENTICULAR CLOUDS

Called lenticular clouds due to their lens-like shape, these unusual clouds are sometimes compared to flying saucers. Some even have iridescent colors around their edges, thanks to a natural process called **irisation**. They form high up in the **atmosphere**, above mountains and other obstacles, but can drift away, maintaining their disk-like shape. Many people believe they're the single best scientific explanation for real-life UFO sightings.

HOLE-PUNCH CLOUDS

Also called a sky-punch, a hole-punch cloud is a large, round gap that can appear in some cloud types. They can form when airplanes pass through altocumulus or cirrocumulus clouds. The aircraft trigger a chain reaction among very small ice crystals, causing them to form heavier crystals. When the ice crystals fall to Earth or liquid water evaporates, they leave a hole in their place.

CONTRAILS

Also caused by aircraft, **contrails** form when hot, humid air from the exhaust of a jet engine mixes with the cooler air of the sky and water droplets form around particles in the exhaust. They look like long, thin lines in the sky, and can go on for miles. The same principle is put to use in skywriting, a process in which aircraft use smoke to write messages thousands of feet up in the air, which can be read from the ground.

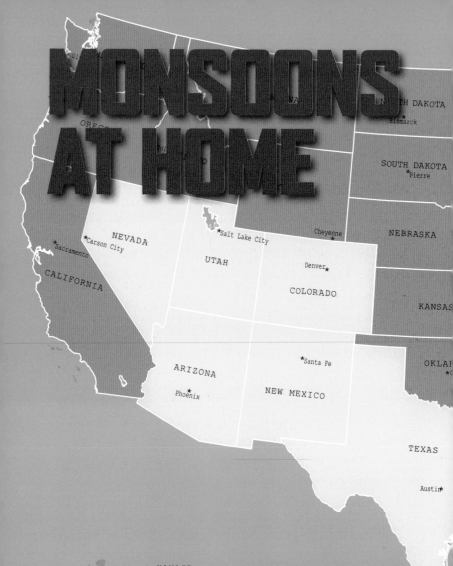

MONSOONS
AT HOME

In the United States, a monsoon season
from June 15 to September 30 each
year sends rain to southwest Texas, New
Mexico, and Arizona, as well as parts of
southern Nevada, Utah, and Colorado.

MINNESOTA

MICHIGAN

MAINE

St Paul

WISCONSIN

Madison
★

Lansing
★

Montpelier ★ Augusta
★

Concord
★

VERMONT

NEW HAMPSHIRE

NEW YORK

Albany
★

Boston
★

MASSACHUSETTS

Providence
★

IOWA

Des Moines
★

Hartford
★

RHODE ISLAND

ILLINOIS

INDIANA

OHIO

Columbus
★

PENNSYLVANIA

Harrisburg
★

Trenton
★

CONNECTICUT

NEW JERSEY

Springfield
★

Indianapolis
★

WEST
VIRGINIA

Annapolis ★ Dover
★

DELAWARE

DC ★ Washington

MARYLAND

MISSOURI

Jefferson City
★

Frankfort
★

Charleston
★

VIRGINIA

Richmond
★

KENTUCKY

Nashville
★

Raleigh
★

TENNESSEE

NORTH CAROLINA

ARKANSAS

Little Rock
★

Columbia
★

SOUTH
CAROLINA

MISSISSIPPI

ALABAMA

Atlanta
★

GEORGIA

Montgomery
★

Jackson
★

LOUISIANA

Baton Rouge
★

Tallahassee
★

ALASKA

Juneau
★

In recent years, the monsoon has led to unprecedented, fatal flooding in Arizona. In September 2014, storms in the Sun Valley area led to flash floods. Up to 200 homes were flooded. At least 24 cars were found underwater on Interstate 10. And 2 people lost their lives.

135

LET IT SNOW!

THE WORLD'S LARGEST SNOWMAN

The world's largest snowman was actually a snowwoman! Built in Bethel, Maine, in 2008, the snowwoman stood 122 feet 1 inch tall and weighed 13 million pounds! Her eyes were 5-feet-tall wreaths, and her eyelashes were made from old skis. She was named Olympia, after one of Maine's senators, Olympia Snowe.

Snow becomes more compact as it approaches its **melting point**. Powder snow, which is light and fluffy, doesn't stick to itself; the stickiness is necessary to mold snow into a shape.

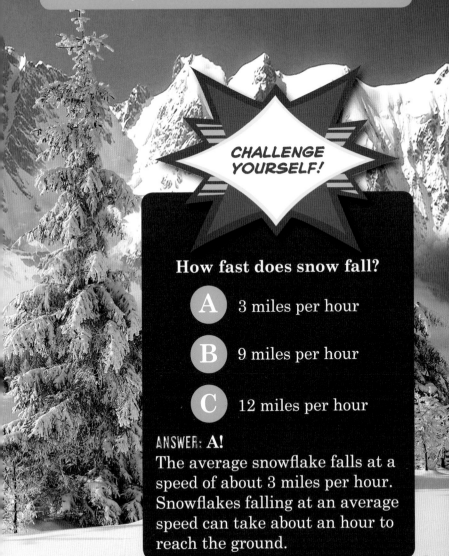

CHALLENGE YOURSELF!

How fast does snow fall?

A 3 miles per hour

B 9 miles per hour

C 12 miles per hour

ANSWER: **A!**
The average snowflake falls at a speed of about 3 miles per hour. Snowflakes falling at an average speed can take about an hour to reach the ground.

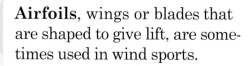

Airfoils, wings or blades that are shaped to give lift, are sometimes used in wind sports.

TAKING OFF FOR THE WEEKEND

Hot-air balloons use fire burners to heat large pockets of air. The balloon system weighs about 2.5 tons, but the 77,550 cubic feet of hot air in the balloon rises in the milder **atmosphere** with enough force to achieve liftoff!

GETTING A RISE OUT OF WEATHER!

Kite jumpers use a large kite to give them lift as they do brief acrobatic tricks.

Paragliding is a cross between parachuting and hang gliding. Paragliders ride mountain updrafts to gain altitude.

PARAGLIDING

PARACHUTING

CRAZY BUT TRUE

Pilots don't generally steer hot-air balloons. Wind does! A pilot's skill is to pick the right altitude to find the right wind.

NOW YOU SEE IT, NOW YOU DON'T.

Have you ever seen a puddle on the road that seems to disappear as your car gets closer? The water doesn't simply dry up. It wasn't there in the first place! A **mirage** is a trick of light, in which very hot air creates the illusion of rippling water.

HOW MIRAGES WORK

Mirages most often appear when the surface of the ground is very, very hot—such as hot asphalt on a summer day, or a stretch of sand in the desert. Hot pockets of air, heated by the ground, cause light to bend at varying angles, which makes fixed straight lines appear moving and wavy. If light is bent enough, it can appear reflective, making an inverted image of the sky or another object farther away—much like a mirror or a puddle of water. The combination of reflection and rippling gives the illusion of pooling water on the ground, off in the distance.

BORN TO BE WILD!

Wildfires are fueled by weather and can cross acres of land in minutes—consuming everything they touch.

During a U.S. **drought** in 1988, 36% of Yellowstone National Park was destroyed or affected by fire.

CRAZY BUT TRUE

Wildfires spread fast—at speeds of up to 14 miles per hour. They can also change direction unexpectedly, jumping over gaps such as roads and rivers.

About 75,000 wildfires burn in the United States every year, burning over 5 million acres of land to the ground. In recent years, drought conditions have increased their burn range to 9 million acres!

CAUSES OF FOREST FIRES

Although 4 out of 5 wildfires are started by people, sometimes all it takes is a **lightning** strike. Wildfires can even be started by volcanic eruptions.

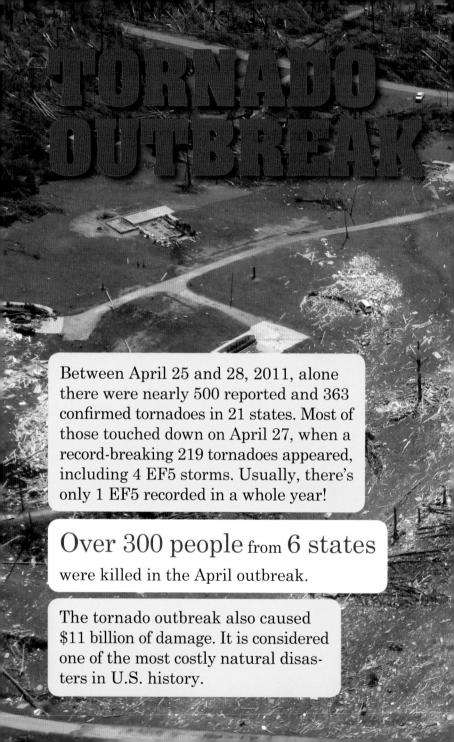

TORNADO OUTBREAK

Between April 25 and 28, 2011, alone there were nearly 500 reported and 363 confirmed tornadoes in 21 states. Most of those touched down on April 27, when a record-breaking 219 tornadoes appeared, including 4 EF5 storms. Usually, there's only 1 EF5 recorded in a whole year!

Over 300 people from 6 states were killed in the April outbreak.

The tornado outbreak also caused $11 billion of damage. It is considered one of the most costly natural disasters in U.S. history.

During that same season, another 158 people were killed by a tornado in Joplin, Missouri, on May 22, 2011. There were more than 1,700 confirmed tornadoes in the United States in 2011, resulting in 553 deaths. That's only 11 fewer than the 10 years before combined!

WINTRY MIX

SLEET

Sleet is rain that freezes on its way to the ground. Not to be confused with freezing rain, which freezes after it hits.

HAIL

Hail is similar to sleet, but larger. Hailstones form when updrafts in a storm force falling pellets of ice back up and into more drops of super-cooled water. The balls of ice grow larger in size the longer they're held aloft.

HAILSTONES

CRAZY BUT TRUE

While hail typically grows to be somewhere between the size of a pea and the size of a marble, the largest hailstone on record was 8 inches wide. It weighed 1 pound 15 ounces. That's roughly the size of a volleyball!

STRONGEST HURRICANE TO DATE

The most intense **hurricane** to hit landfall in the United States is called the Labor Day Hurricane. It hit the Florida Keys on September 2, 1935. There were sustained winds of 200 miles per hour for several hours. The storm destroyed most local buildings, as well as the Florida East Coast Railway. It killed more than 400 people.

LABOR DAY HURRICANE

BIGGEST KILLERS

In 1900, a hurricane hit Galveston, Texas, killing between 6,000 and 12,000 people—more than a quarter of the island's population. The Category 4 hurricane had wind speeds of over 120 miles per hour and carried with it a 15-foot **storm surge** that leveled nearly everything in town. All told, the hurricane did $20 million of damage, considerably more in today's money. It is considered the deadliest natural disaster ever to strike the United States.

The most devastating **tropical cyclone** of all, however, hit East Pakistan (in present-day Bangladesh) and part of India in 1970, flooding the densely populated Ganges Delta, killing up to 500,000 people.

NOR'EASTERS

Nor'easters are giant winter storm systems that affect the East Coast of the United States and Canada. They get their name from the direction the wind is coming from: the northeast.

Sometimes forming over Atlantic coastal waters, nor'easter storms are infamous for producing heavy snowfall, rain, and destructive waves. The powerful surf can cause severe beach erosion and coastal flooding.

CRAZY BUT TRUE

Wind gusts associated with a nor'easter can be even stronger than those of a **hurricane**!

Like hurricanes, nor'easters are fueled by warm, humid air from the Atlantic. They form areas of low **air pressure** as well as cyclones of winter weather.

SUPER BLIZZARDS!

Perhaps the largest **blizzard** in North America in recent history was a nor'easter-type blizzard nicknamed Snowmageddon. It struck the East Coast in February 2010, but had far-reaching weather effects, including extensive flooding and **landslides** in Mexico.

The Great Blizzard of 1888 was a nor'easter. It was one of the worst blizzards in history. It dropped between 40 and 50 inches of snow in some places and had sustained freezing winds of more than 45 miles per hour. The snowstorm killed 400 people, mostly in New York.

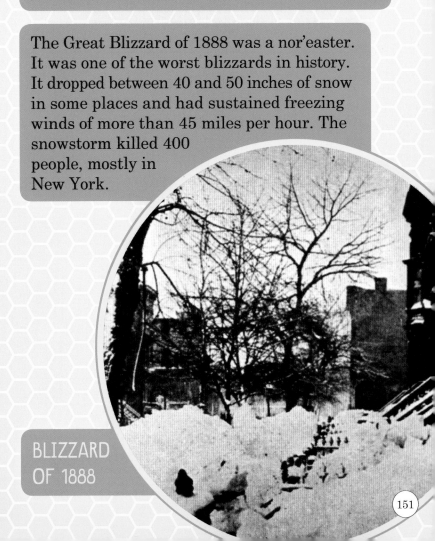

BLIZZARD OF 1888

Between 6 and 9 miles off the ground, high up in the **atmosphere**, there are fast-flowing air currents. Each is generally thousands of miles long, but relatively thin. Together, these rapid rivers of air are called the **jet stream**.

The Northern Hemisphere and the Southern Hemisphere each have two individual currents. One is a polar jet, and the other is a subtropical jet.

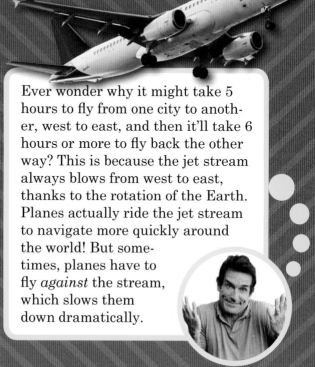

Ever wonder why it might take 5 hours to fly from one city to another, west to east, and then it'll take 6 hours or more to fly back the other way? This is because the jet stream always blows from west to east, thanks to the rotation of the Earth. Planes actually ride the jet stream to navigate more quickly around the world! But sometimes, planes have to fly *against* the stream, which slows them down dramatically.

CRAZY BUT TRUE

The jet stream was discovered thanks to a volcanic eruption! In 1883, the Krakatoa volcano in the area we now call Indonesia spewed a massive amount of smoke and dust into the atmosphere. But instead of dispersing evenly throughout the air, it flowed in high channels—effectively drawing the first map of the jet stream.

KRAKATOA

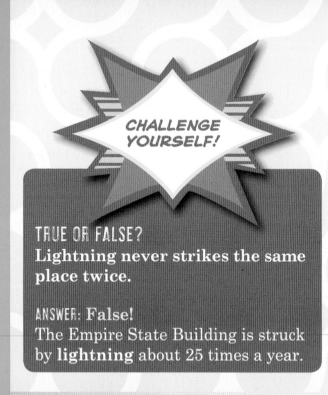

LIGHTNING STRIKE

CHALLENGE YOURSELF!

TRUE OR FALSE?
Lightning never strikes the same place twice.

ANSWER: False!
The Empire State Building is struck by **lightning** about 25 times a year.

EMPIRE STATE BUILDING

LIGHTNING

About 50 people in the United States die each year due to lightning strikes, and hundreds more are injured.

The chance of being struck by lightning in the States is 1 in 960,000 in a given year.

SURVIVING A HURRICANE

Not all **hurricanes** make landfall. And though only the strongest of them do serious damage, no storm should be taken too lightly.

MARK YOUR CALENDAR!

Hurricane season lasts from June 1 to November 30.

KNOW THE WARNING SIGNS

A hurricane watch is issued for coastal areas where hurricane conditions are possible within 48 hours. People who live in the affected area are warned to take protective measures, especially those who live on or near the water.

A hurricane warning, on the other hand, is issued only when hurricane-strength winds are expected to hit within 36 hours. People in the warning area should evacuate and head for safety.

GETTING READY

Before a hurricane, people prepare by boarding up their windows and securing objects that might otherwise blow away. They stock up on food, water, and other supplies—in case they're unable to leave their shelter for days. Preparations are made in case the power goes out.

During a hurricane, people are urged to stay indoors.

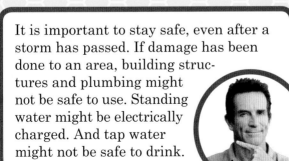

It is important to stay safe, even after a storm has passed. If damage has been done to an area, building structures and plumbing might not be safe to use. Standing water might be electrically charged. And tap water might not be safe to drink.

HOW HURRICANES GET THEIR NAMES

The World Meteorological Organization (WMO) has used a variation of the same method of naming **tropical cyclones** since 1953. There are 6 lists of 21 names, representing the letters of the alphabet (Q, U, X, Y, and Z are excluded). The lists are used in rotation, so that the names used in 2017 will be used again in 2023!

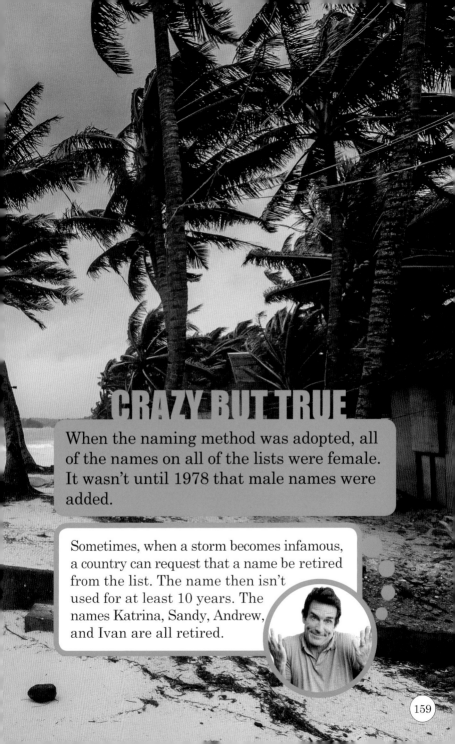

CRAZY BUT TRUE

When the naming method was adopted, all of the names on all of the lists were female. It wasn't until 1978 that male names were added.

Sometimes, when a storm becomes infamous, a country can request that a name be retired from the list. The name then isn't used for at least 10 years. The names Katrina, Sandy, Andrew, and Ivan are all retired.

Weather is ever-changing and scientists are making new discoveries all the time. What will our weather be like in 10 years? 50 years? 100 years? What do you predict?

GLOSSARY

ACID RAIN: rain that contains acids that form in the atmosphere, often caused by environmental pollution

AIRFOIL: a winglike structure, such as a sail, that provides lift when moved through air

AIR MASS: a relatively large body of air in the atmosphere with uniform temperature and moisture

AIR PRESSURE: the force exerted on an area by the weight of air above it

ATMOSPHERE: the layer of gases surrounding the planet, held in place by gravity

AURORA: a natural light display caused by charged particles from the sun that glow as they enter the atmosphere

BLIZZARD: a severe snowstorm characterized by strong winds over a relatively long period of time, heavy snow, and reduced visibility

CLIMATE: the average pattern of weather in a particular place over a long period of time

CLOUD SEEDING: the introduction of particles to a cloud, usually in the hopes of producing rain

CONTRAILS: long, thin clouds that form when aircraft exhaust cools in the atmosphere

DEW: water droplets that form in nature due to condensation

DEW POINT: the temperature at which dew droplets form out of a particular air mass

DOPPLER RADAR: a tracking system that uses the Doppler effect to determine the speed and motion of distant objects

DROUGHT: an extended period of dryness resulting from abnormally low amounts of precipitation

EQUATOR: an imaginary line halfway between the Earth's North and South Poles, dividing the planet into the Northern and Southern Hemispheres

FIRE WHIRL: a twisting vortex of fire and ash, caused when winds and rising heat combine and suck up debris and combustible gases

HEAT WAVE: an extended period of unusually hot weather

HUMIDITY: the amount of water vapor in the air

HURRICANE: a violent tropical cyclone with storm winds of at least 74 miles per hour

IRISATION: a light phenomenon in the Earth's atmosphere in which diffracted sunlight through clouds produces a mixture of iridescent colors

JET STREAM: a fast-flowing river of air found in the Earth's atmosphere

LANDSLIDE: a mass movement of rock, soil, and debris down a slope

LEVEE: a physical structure, such as a wall, built to prevent flooding

LIGHTNING: the sudden discharge of electricity during a thunderstorm

MELTING POINT: the temperature at which a solid becomes a liquid

MESOCYCLONE: the central vortex of air within a large storm

METEOROLOGY: the study of the atmosphere, including weather

MIRAGE: the optical illusion of a reflection caused by atmospheric conditions

MUDSLIDE: a mass movement of mud and other material down a slope

NOR'EASTER: a huge storm system that moves along the East Coast of North America, blowing from a northeasterly direction

OZONE: an unstable molecule of oxygen atoms, which can be created by lightning

PRECIPITATION: water that falls to the ground in the form of rain, snow, sleet, or hail

SEA LEVEL: the average level of the sea's surface, from which height and elevation can be measured

SNOWDRIFT: a mound-shaped pile of snow formed by wind

SOLAR RADIATION: energy emitted from the sun

STORM SURGE: the abnormal rapid rise in water level caused by a storm

THUNDER: the loud noise generated by lightning, caused by the rapid expansion of air as it is heated

TROPICAL CYCLONE: a storm with strong winds circulating an area of low pressure

TROPICAL DEPRESSION: a low-pressure area combined with thunderstorms that creates circular wind flow originating in tropical areas

TROPOSPHERE: the lowest layer of the Earth's atmosphere, where most weather occurs

TSUNAMI: seismic sea waves, caused by underwater earthquakes, landslides, or volcanic eruptions

WATER VAPOR: the gaseous state of water, formed when water evaporates

WATERSPOUT: a tornado that forms over a body of water

WAVELENGTH: the distance between two identical parts of a waveform, such as the crests

WILDFIRE: a large-scale, uncontrolled fire that can spread rapidly in the wilderness

INDEX   Numbers in *italics* refer to illustrations